TI IREE THIEVES
BOOK SIX

The Dark Island

Kids Can Press acknowledges the financial support of the Government of Ontario, through the Ontario Media Development Corporation's Ontario Book Initiative; the Ontario Arts Council; the Canada Council for the Arts; and the Government of Canada, through the CBF, for our publishing activity.

Published in Canada by
Kids Can Press Ltd.
25 Dockside Drive
Toronto, ON M5A 0B5

Published in the U.S. by
Kids Can Press Ltd.
2250 Military Road
Tonawanda, NY 14150

www.kidscanpress.com

Edited by Yasemin Uçar
Designed by Scott Chantler and Michael Reis
Pages lettered with Blambot comic fonts

The hardcover edition of this book is smyth sewn casebound.
The paperback edition of this book is limp sewn with a drawn-on cover.
Manufactured in Buji, Shenzhen, China, in 10/2015 by WKT Company

CM 16 0 9 8 7 6 5 4 3 2 1
CM PA 16 0 9 8 7 6 5 4 3 2 1

Library and Archives Canada Cataloguing in Publication

Chantler, Scott, author, artist
      The dark island / Scott Chantler.

(Three thieves book 6)
ISBN 978-1-894786-55-3 (bound)   ISBN 978-1-894786-56-0 (pbk.)

      1. Graphic novels. I. Title. II. Series: Chantler, Scott.
Three thieves ; bk. 6.

PN6733.C53D37 2016   j741.5'971   C2015-903359-4

Kids Can Press is a *Corus*™ Entertainment company

THREE THIEVES
BOOK SIX

The Dark Island

SCOTT CHANTLER

Kids Can Press

ACT ONE

Flight

THIS BOY IS NOT YOUR SON.

NOT MY OWN FLESH AND BLOOD, NO...

BUT HE'S MY SON AS SURELY AS NORKERS HAVE NOSES.

CAPTAIN...?

HOW LONG HAS HE BEEN HERE?

NINE WINTERS NOW, I GUESS...

WHAT'S ALL THIS ABOUT?

LISTEN, BOY. DID YOU HAVE A SISTER? BEFORE YOU CAME HERE? A *TWIN*?

8

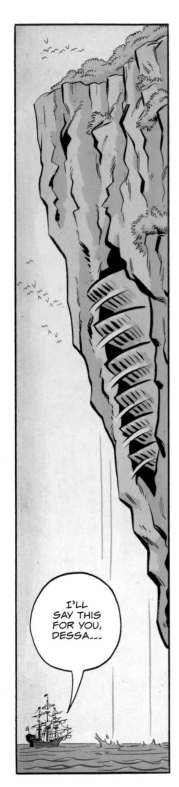

10

YOU JUST BETTER HOPE WE DON'T END UP NEEDING THEM ON THE RETURN VOYAGE.

YOU'RE CONFIDENT THESE THINGS WILL *ACTUALLY* FLY?

THEY WILL...

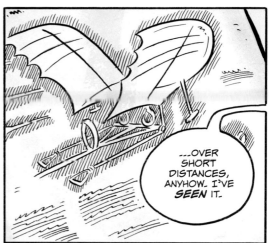

...OVER SHORT DISTANCES, ANYHOW. I'VE *SEEN* IT.

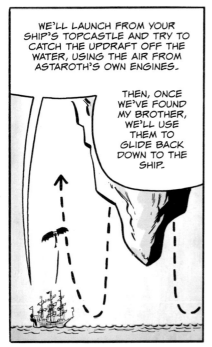

WE'LL LAUNCH FROM YOUR SHIP'S TOPCASTLE AND TRY TO CATCH THE UPDRAFT OFF THE WATER, USING THE AIR FROM ASTAROTH'S OWN ENGINES.

THEN, ONCE WE'VE FOUND MY BROTHER, WE'LL USE THEM TO GLIDE BACK DOWN TO THE SHIP.

DO YOU WANT TO COME WITH US? WE COULD MAKE ONE OF THESE FOR *YOU.*

HA!

YOU'D NOT GET ME INTO ONE OF THOSE CONTRAPTIONS FOR ALL THE GOLD IN THE SIX KINGDOMS, ETTIN.

THE HEAVENS ARE FOR ANGELS. I'LL TAKE MY CHANCES DOWN HERE ON THE SEA, WHERE I BELONG.

JUST REMEMBER OUR AGREEMENT...

...ANY TREASURE YOU FIND UP THERE IS *MINE*—PAYMENT FOR YOUR PASSAGE, AND FOR FREEING YOU FROM THOSE TWO-BIT SMUGGLERS.

PFFT. THAT'S WHAT *SHE* THINKS.

GOT MY LUCKY LOCKPICKS RIGHT HERE, LADY PIRATE QUEEN, MA'AM!

ASSUMING I GET A CHANCE TO USE 'EM AND DON'T LAND FACE DOWN IN THE OCEAN.

YOU SAYING YOU DON'T THINK THIS'LL WORK?

I'M SAYING *YOU'RE* GOING FIRST.

GLADLY.

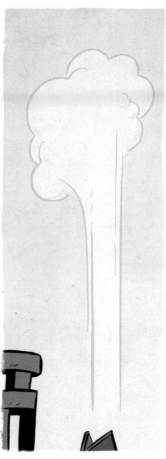

13

LOOK!

NOT TO MENTION THE LEGENDARY *TREASURE OF ASTAROTH!*

WHAT? THE MISSING BROTHER THING IS *YOUR* RACKET. MINE IS STEALING STUFF.

WHATEVER WE'RE LOOKIN' FOR, LET'S BE CAREFUL. DON'T FORGET THE RUMORS.

PFFT. THERE'S NO SUCH THING AS DEMONS, FISK. WE'LL BE FINE.

WHATEVER'S ON THIS ISLAND CAN'T BE *NEARLY* AS BAD AS WHAT WE'VE BEEN THROUGH TO GET HERE.

I HAVE A FEELING THE WORST IS BEHIND US.

ACT TWO

Blind Man's Bluff

WHERE ARE YOU TAKING ME? I WANT TO GO BACK TO MY FATHER!

Loggerhea

Hanbroo

THAT MAN IS NO MORE YOUR FATHER THAN I AM. NOW KEEP QUIET.

IS IT REALLY NECESSARY TO KEEP THE BOY BOUND, CAPTAIN?

YES.

ALL THAT GIRL WANTS IN THE WORLD IS TO HAVE HER BROTHER BACK...

AS LONG AS WE DON'T LET HIM GET AWAY, *SHE'LL* COME TO *US.*

I *TOLD* YOU, I DON'T *HAVE* A...

...FOR.

HELLO.

29

WHAT'S YOUR NAME, LITTLE ONE?

TAFARI.

TAFARI, MY NAME IS DESSA. AND THESE ARE MY FRIENDS TOPPER AND FISK.

HI.

NOW THIS BOY WHO WAS HERE. WAS HIS NAME JARED? DID HE LOOK LIKE ME? RED HAIR, FRECKLES?

NO.

I TOLD YOU. HIS NAME WAS OLIVAR...

...AND HE DIDN'T LOOK LIKE YOU AT ALL.

WHAT ELSE CAN YOU TELL US ABOUT YOUR SISTER?

NOTHING...

SKRITCH
SKRITCH
SKRITCH

I-I DIDN'T EVEN REMEMBER I HAD ONE.

WELL, DON'T GET USED TO IT...

ONCE WE BRING HER BACK TO KINGSBRIDGE, THE QUEEN WILL SEE THAT THE HANGMAN FINALLY GETS HER.

SKRITCH

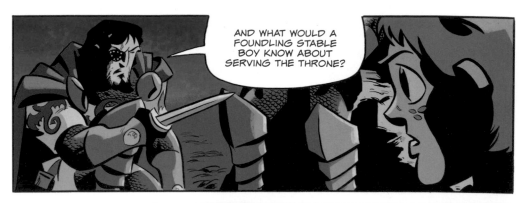

AND WHAT WOULD A FOUNDLING STABLE BOY KNOW ABOUT SERVING THE THRONE?

ONLY THAT WHILE YOU DRAGONS SHOULD HAVE BEEN PROTECTING THE KING, YOU WERE TOO BUSY *KIDNAPPING* A LITTLE BOY AND *BURNING HIS MOTHER'S HOUSE DOWN!*

WAS *ANYONE* GUARDING THE KING?

I WAS.

SKRITCH
SKRITCH

WAIT.

WHOOSH

YOU WERE KIDNAPPED BY THE **KING'S DRAGONS?**

YES.

ON THE NIGHT KING RODERICK WAS MURDERED?

Y-YES.

WAS THERE ANOTHER MAN ALSO...?

WE'RE ALMOST THERE!

MAYBE THE TOYMAKER WILL LET YOU THREE LIVE WITH US! WE EACH HAVE A ROOM FILLED WITH SPECIAL THINGS JUST FOR *US!*

I CAN ASK HIM, NEXT TIME HE SHOWS UP!

THIS TOYMAKER GUY ISN'T ALWAYS AROUND?

HE LIVES INSIDE THE BIG TREE. HE ONLY COMES OUT SOMETIMES. BUT HE SAYS HE'S ALWAYS WATCHING US.

IS HE NOW?

I JUST WANT TO TAKE A LOOK AROUND, TAFARI. I'M NOT PLANNING ON STAYING.

YOU'LL PROBABLY CHANGE YOUR MIND WHEN YOU SEE *THIS*---

<GASP!>

TAFARI! THERE YOU ARE!

WE'RE PLAYING BLIND MAN'S BLUFF! SHIZU IS "IT" AND—

!

W-WHO ARE THEY?

THEY'RE MY NEW FRIENDS! I MET THEM IN THE JUNGLE.

BUT...

...HOW DID THEY GET THERE?

WHAT ELSE DO YOU REMEMBER, BOY?

I...I'M THINKING...

DO IT *FASTER.*

THE MAN...HIS NAME WAS—

GREYFALCON.

YES.

"HE TOOK ME TO A RUIN...

...WHERE WE MET THREE LITTLE MEN."

YOU PLAYIN' NURSEMAID NOW, GREYFALCON?

NEVER MIND.

WHAT ABOUT THE *LETTER?*

WAIT.

HE ASKED ABOUT A *LETTER?*

YES....

"...BUT THEY DIDN'T HAVE IT. THEY TOLD HIM THEY COULDN'T FIND IT."

NO MATTER.

AND THAT WAS THE LAST I HEARD OF IT.

HOW *DID* YOU THREE GET HERE? DID THE TOYMAKER BRING YOU?

NOBODY "BROUGHT" US.

WE CAME ON OUR OWN, LOOKING FOR MY BROTHER. HIS NAME IS JARED.

THEN YOU'VE COME TO THE WRONG PLACE....

NOBODY'S BROTHER HERE.

JUST TAFARI, MARIGOLD AND ME.

WHAT ABOUT THE TOYMAKER?

HIM, TOO, SOMETIMES.

HE COMES OUT OF THERE. HE ALWAYS HAS SOMETHING AMAZING FOR US!

43

TELL US MORE.

TH-THERE *IS* NO MORE.

OF COURSE THERE IS. *THINK*, BOY!

THERE...

"...THERE WAS *ANOTHER* MAN."

THE STABLEMAN.

NO.

THIS WAS BEFORE THAT...

"I WAS ASLEEP, AND THEIR VOICES WOKE ME UP.

DID ANYONE SEE HIM?

NO MATTER...

YOU AND I ARE THE ONLY ONES OUTSIDE THE PALACE WHO KNOW WHO HE IS.

46

47

---IF THE TOYMAKER LIVES INSIDE THE TREE, WHERE DO YOU GIRLS LIVE?

IN THE OTHER TREES, SILLY.

YOU MEAN IN THOSE HUTS?

BUT WHY ARE THERE *SIX* OF THEM, IF THERE'S ONLY *THREE* OF YOU?

THAT ONE WAS OLIVAR'S. BUT HE'S GONE NOW.

BUT WHERE WOULD HE GO?

WHAT DID HE *DO*, ANYWAY?

HE ASKED *TOO MANY QUESTIONS.*

WHAT ABOUT THE OTHER TWO, THEN?

THAT ONE'S EMPTY. ALWAYS HAS BEEN.

AND THE OTHER?

IT'S OUR LIBRARY!

THE TOYMAKER FILLED IT WITH BOOKS!

DID YOU SAY *BOOKS?*

PALADIN.

THIS HUT WAS MEANT FOR PALADIN.

WHAT'S A "PALADIN"?

HE'S THE CROWN PRINCE OF MEDORIA.

WHO *ARE* YOU THREE?

SO HOW DID YOU COME TO LIVE WITH THE STABLEMAN?

I DON'T REMEMBER. HE AND HIS WIFE ALWAYS TOLD ME THEY FOUND ME BY THE ROADSIDE.

"THEY HAD NO CHILDREN OF THEIR OWN, SO THEY TOOK ME IN.

"I LIVED WITH THEM AND WORKED IN THEIR STABLE. THEY WERE KIND TO ME, AND I WAS SAFE AND HAPPY..."

SO I GUESS I MADE MYSELF FORGET EVERYTHING THAT HAD HAPPENED BEFORE.

UNTIL TODAY.

YOU'LL COME TO NO HARM IN OUR CARE, JARED.

IS THAT WHAT YOU TOLD THE KING?

52

I **TOLD** YOU! I'M A PRINCESS!

YOU STOP WITH THAT PRINCESS TALK, OR HE'LL TAKE **YOU** AWAY NEXT.

NO...

...I MEAN WHERE DID YOU COME FROM?

"COME FROM"...?

JUST IGNORE MARIGOLD. SHE'S BEEN HERE SINCE SHE WAS A BABY, AND THINKS THE ISLAND IS THE **WHOLE WORLD.**

YOU CAN'T PROVE THAT IT ISN'T!

WHERE DO YOU THINK **THEY** CAME FROM, MUTTONHEAD?

AND DID GREYFALCON BRING YOU ALL HERE?

I DON'T KNOW WHO THAT IS.

THE TOYMAKER BROUGHT US.

I'LL TAKE THAT AS A YES.

BECAUSE I'M PRETTY CERTAIN THAT GREYFALCON AND THIS TOYMAKER OF YOURS ARE ONE AND THE SAME.

WHERE ARE YOU *GOING?!*

TO MAKE HIM TELL ME WHERE MY BROTHER IS. THEN I'M BUSTING YOU THREE OUT OF THIS PRISON.

"PRISON"?!

LOOK AROUND YOU! IT'S *PARADISE!*

SHE'S RIGHT! IT'S *FUN* HERE!

WHY DO YOU THINK SOMEONE WOULD PUT YOU WAY OUT HERE AT THE *EDGE OF THE WORLD?!*

SO THAT YOU *CAN'T LEAVE!*

WHO WOULD *WANT* TO?

OLIVAR WANTED TO.

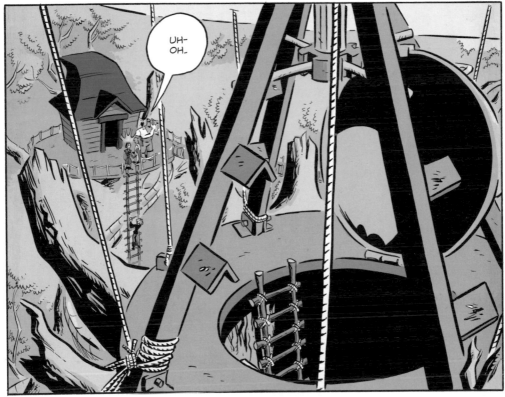

THE BOY'S STORY IS REMARKABLE, TO SAY THE LEAST...

Z

DO YOU BELIEVE ANY OF IT?

EVERY WORD.

ME, TOO, I'M AFRAID.

WHAT DO YOU THINK IT ALL MEANS?

WHAT'S SO SPECIAL ABOUT HIM THAT GREYFALCON WANTED TO HIDE HIM AWAY?

I DON'T KNOW...

Z

BUT YOU CAN BET I KNOW WHO TO *ASK.*

56

ACT THREE

The Demon

W-WHERE DID YOU COME FROM?

IT'S A LONG STORY.

BUT NOW THAT I'VE FREED YOU...

KLIK

...YOU CAN REPAY ME BY TELLING ME WHERE THE TREASURE IS HIDDEN.

"TREASURE"...?

THERE'S NO TREASURE HERE.

BUT I'M SURE MY FAMILY WILL PAY YOU HANDSOMELY FOR MY SAFE RETURN...

...I'M THE CROWN PRINCE OF LOTHAR.

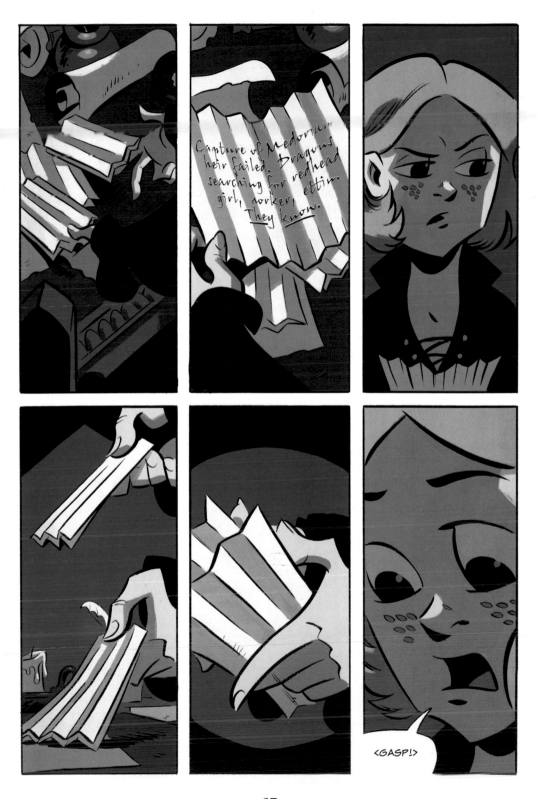

67

In Loggerhead, with Dragons. Girl hired ship. If she arrives before we do— KILL HER.

KILL HER.

WE NEED TO FIND TOPPER...

IT'S TIME TO GO.

SO TAFARI WAS RIGHT. EVERYONE HERE REALLY *IS* A PRINCE OR PRINCESS.

YES.

SHE'S THE HEIR OF KAMARIA. MARIGOLD IS THE PRINCESS OF MAGISHEAD. AND SHIZU IS A DAUGHTER OF THE EMPEROR OF GAN

THEN WHAT ARE YOU ALL DOING *HERE?*

THE TOYMAKER KIDNAPPED US.

HE HOPED HIS ISLAND OF WONDERS WOULD MAKE US FORGET WHO WE WERE AND WHERE WE CAME FROM. BUT THE OLDER I GOT, THE MORE I REALIZED SOMETHING WAS WRONG.

I THINK HE'S TRYING TO USE THE FOUR OF US TO MANIPULATE THE THRONES OF OUR KINGDOMS IN SOME WAY.

WE NEED TO TELL DESSA.

UM... WHY HAVE WE...

...STOPPED?

I DARE NOT EVEN GUESS HOW YOU MANAGED TO GET TO THIS ISLAND, NORKER...

...BUT I ASSURE YOU, NO ONE HAS EVER *LEFT* IT.

NOR EVER *WILL.*

NO!

AND THAT INCLUDES YOUR *TWO* FRIENDS.

DESSA! FISK!

RUN!

TOPPER....?

LET'S GET OUT OF HERE.

BUT HE'S IN TROUBLE!

AND HE TRIED TO SAVE *US* WITH A WARNING, DESSA.

THERE ARE THOSE LITTLE ONES TO THINK ABOUT....

WE CAN STILL HELP *THEM.*

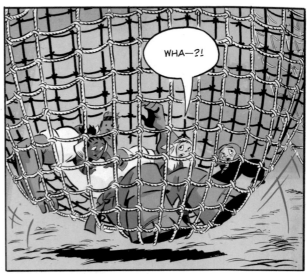

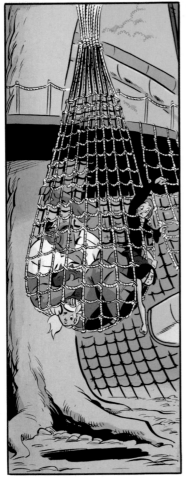

SSSSSSSSSSSSSSSSSSSSSSSS

KLAK

Flik

WHOOOOOOOOOOOOOOOOOOSH

IT'S THE BEGGARS-CAN'T-BE-CHOOSERS KIND, YOUR HIGHNESS. <KOFF!>

<KOFF! KOFF!> WHAT KIND OF RESCUE *IS* THIS, EXACTLY?

ALSO THE PIPE-DOWN-AND-KEEP-CLIMBING KIND. <KOFF!>

80

WE'RE TRAPPED!

THAT'S WHAT I'VE BEEN TRYING TO *TELL* YOU THREE!

DESSA....!

LOOK!

GREYFALCON.

DESSA!

83

W-WHERE'S HE GOING?

ISN'T HE GOING TO TAKE US *WITH* HIM? DOESN'T HE CARE ABOUT US ANYMORE?

I'M NOT SURE HOW MUCH HE CARED ABOUT US TO BEGIN WITH, MARIGOLD.

WHAT DID YOU DO WITH HIM, YOU MONSTER?!

WHOOOOSH

UH-OH.

86

WHUMP

YOU THINK THE GIRL WAS COMING HERE TO LOGGERHEAD?

SHE'D NEED A SHIP TO GET TO ASTAROTH. THIS IS THE PLACE TO FIND ONE.

OI! YOU!

BETTER HURRY OR YE'LL MISS YER BOAT!

I BEG YOUR PARDON?

YER WITH THE OTHER REDCAPES, AIN'T YE?

YOU'VE SEEN THE REST OF OUR ORDER?

SURE I SEEN 'EM.

THEY'RE SETTIN' SAIL ABOARD THE *WIND PEARL* AS WE SPEAK.

RIDE, PHINEAS!

!?!

CAPTAIN!

<KOFF! KOFF!>

YOU STILL HERE?

OLIVAR!

GO BACK DOWN. NOTHIN' OUT HERE BUT FIRE.

NOTHIN' DOWN THERE BUT STUFF THAT BURNS.

ANYONE NEED A RIDE?

GRAB ON TO SOMETHING!

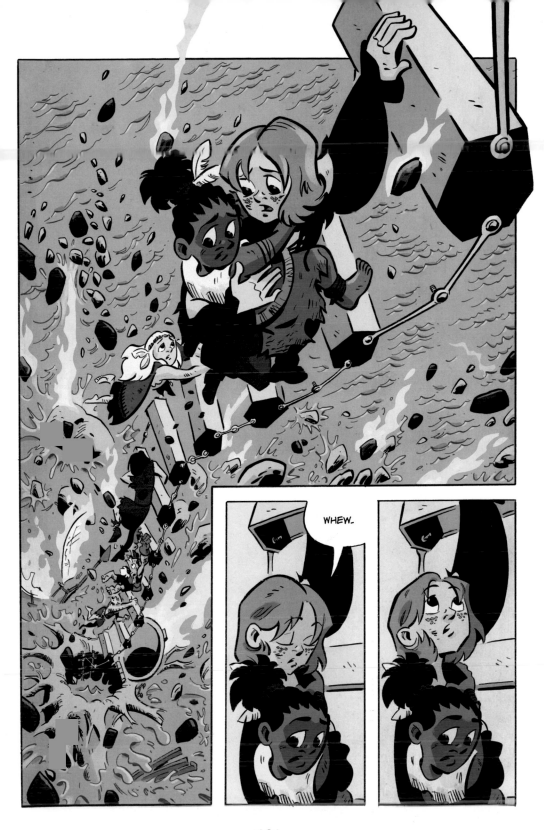

DRAKE! JUST IN TIME!

THE GIRL SAILED FROM THIS PORT A FORTNIGHT AGO...

WE'VE COMMANDEERED THIS SHIP AND HER CREW TO CHASE HER DOW—

!

FOUND HIM, SIR!

<GASP!>

WHO IS *THIS?*

I WAS GOING TO ASK *YOU* THE SAME QUESTION.

SOMETHING TOLD ME YOU MIGHT KNOW.

YOU'RE IN OVER YOUR HEAD HERE, DRAKE...

HAND THE BOY OVER.

NO.

WELL, HELLO, JARED...

LOOK!

CLIMB DOWN! YOU'LL BE ABLE TO DROP ONTO THE SHIP!

AREN'T YOU COMING?

IF I LET GO....

THEN HOW ARE YOU GOING TO—?

NO–

GET THOSE LITTLE ONES TO THEIR FAMILIES WHERE THEY BELONG, DESSA...

NO, FISK...!

THIS IS ALL MY FAULT! JARED WASN'T EVEN HERE AND I—

DESSA, COME ON!

GO, DESSA!

I CAN'T HOLD IT!

WHUMP

WYETH! HARD ABOUT! FULL SAIL!

114

Praise for the Three Thieves series

Tower of Treasure
★ Winner of the Joe Shuster Award, Comics for Kids

★ "Thrilling action sequences that don't sacrifice sense for simple in the kind
of fantasy tale that can be relished by children of all ages."
— *Quill & Quire*, starred review

"An entertaining and action packed new fantasy adventure series."
— *Publishers Weekly*

The Sign of the Black Rock
"An animated, breathlessly paced adventure that's just hitting its stride."
— *Kirkus Reviews*

"Touches of zany slapstick balance nicely with Dessa's continued resolve
to find her lost brother, and Chantler's inviting cartooning captures
it all with special aplomb." — *Booklist*

The Captive Prince
"Nary a dull moment, nor even a slow one in this escapade's latest outing."
— *Kirkus Reviews*

"… heaps of charm … snappy, colorful artwork … this one can stand well on
its own, though it successfully expands on the growing epic." — *Booklist*

The King's Dragon
"Chantler's cartooning remains sharp, lively, and inviting, and his eye
for rousing action sequences is top-notch. But it's his skill as a
writer that shines through." — *Booklist*

"In his cleanly drawn action sequences, Chantler ingeniously links
present and past with parallel acts or dialogue … adds further depth to a
particularly well-wrought tale." — *Kirkus Reviews*

Pirates of the Silver Coast
"The action is pretty much nonstop, the dialogue is spot on
and the pacing is perfect." — *Chicago Tribune*

"An already classic series. More than enough action, adventure and
clever plot turns to keep a reader turning pages, but most importantly the
story has heart. A lively, inventive and enthralling tale — a must read!"
— Arthur Slade, author of *Dust*

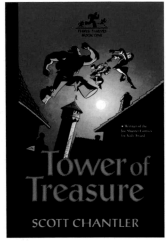

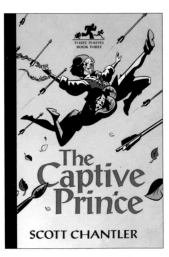
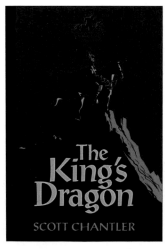
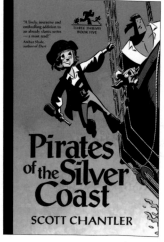